CHRONICLE SERIES

BANFF
THE STORY AND THE SIGHTS

by

Barry Bondar

Whitecap Books
NORTH VANCOUVER, B.C., CANADA

THE DISCOVERY

THE RAILWAY CONSTRUCTION job had been long and difficult. But now, in the fall of 1883, the Canadian Pacific Railway had broken the backbone of the mountains. The opportunity to look for that elusive metal—gold—had finally arrived for three young railway workers.

Frank McCabe and Tom and Bill McCardell set out on yet another prospecting trip. This time, they selected a rather insignificant looking mountain with some hopeful geological signs. After rafting across the Bow River, the men disembarked near one of the many streams flowing into the river. This one, however, was quite different. The water was warm.

The curious men followed the stream to its source—a small basin of sulphur water choked with logs. And just a short distance away, the foul, rotten-egg odour of sulphur rose from an ominous opening in the ground. After much discussion and with great trepidation, one of the three descended through the opening. The flames of the torch lit up a small cave which held clusters of stalactites like "great gleaming jewels" and a small, warm, emerald green pool.

The young men had found a gold mine of a very different sort. The financial advantages of the discovery were immediately apparent. The Cave and Basin Springs would not only soothe the tired muscles of railway workers—for a price—but would attract people with ailments from all over the world in search of the cure that the sulphur waters were purported to provide.

Unfortunately, the lucky prospectors were poor businessmen. It required only a few mistakes in trying to obtain ownership before word of the

First shack at the site of the springs, built by McCabe and the McCardell brothers, 1883.

discovery was common knowledge. The smell of money, it appeared, was as strong as the smell of sulphur in the springs. Soon a confusing array of claims and counterclaims landed upon the desk of the Superintendent of Mines.

His recommendation was clear: create a public reserve around the springs. It was a suggestion warmly received by Ottawa, for the government found in this proposal a partial cure to its own problems. In order to ensure the survival of a young nation called Canada, the government had been forced to undertake one of the largest engineering projects in the history of this nation—the construction of a national railway through some of the most difficult terrain in the world. The cost of construction had proven to be a major financial drain. The economy was very shaky.

The Cave and Basin, however, was an opportunity to help support the new railway and ease the pressures upon the thin strands of Confederation. By developing tourist resorts in the western mountains, the railway could be assured of ongoing revenues. As Sir John A. MacDonald succinctly put it, "These springs will recuperate the patient and recoup the treasury."

The Basin swimming area, ca. 1890.

BUILDING A PARK

AFTER MCCABE AND the McCardells received some financial compensation, the government set aside 25 square kilometres around the springs on November 25, 1885. Expanded and renamed Rocky Mountains Park two years later, Canada's first national park had a very clear function—it was to earn money. It was to be a cooperative business enterprise centred around the development of a unique resort and sanitarium catering to railway patrons.

The government, in close cooperation with the C.P.R., immediately set about to "build" a park. Modelled after contemporary European and American parks, the new park was to be tidy, attractive, and entertaining. This meant the construction of opulent hotels and restaurants, the development of hot springs spas, the careful planting and tending of gardens, and the development of major recreational facilities.

The construction was successful. Rocky Mountains Park became one of Canada's best-known tourist resort areas. It was most definitely not a wilderness preserve. Indeed, this concept was entirely inconsistent with the realities of the day. Wilderness was more than abundant and was certainly in no need of protection. Income generation, not wilderness preservation, was to be the goal.

Banff Avenue, 1887.

It was the dream of the vice-president of the C.P.R. —William Van Horne —to provide deluxe accommodation in some of the most spectacular areas of the Rocky Mountains. The original Banff Springs Hotel, completed in 1888, was made of wood and was the largest hotel in the world at the time. The buildings were subsequently faced with stone taken from Mount Rundle.

Banff Avenue looking towards Cascade Mountain ca. late 1880s.

The opening celebrations of the Grand View Villa. Note the sign on the horse blanket proclaiming "Hot Springs Grand View Bus Line," and the sign on the building advertising "ice cold temperance drinks." Ca. late 1800s.

*Banff was recognized internationally as a recreational paradise
and Tom Wilson's pack trains were an indispensible means of
getting visitors into the back country.*

Members of an expedition in camp near Waterford Lake, 1902. Prof. J. Norman Collie (with binoculars) discovered the Columbia Icefield.

Catch of 35 fish at Lake Minnewanka, ca. 1893.

THE CONSERVATION MOVEMENT

DURING THE FIRST decade of the twentieth century, a new philosophy began to make its presence felt—conservation. Conservation, in reality, was two competing movements. For some, the concept involved the preservation of wilderness for its intrinsic, intangible values. For most, however, conservation involved the setting aside of vast tracts of land for controlled resource exploitation that ensured the greatest possible returns over the greatest period of time.

It was this latter concept that prevailed. With the dramatic expansion of park boundaries, there was a major increase in the types of activities within those boundaries. Rocky Mountains Park was no longer just a tourist resort. It had now become the home of

resource-based industries and projects including large-scale coal mining operations, hydroelectric developments, and extensive logging operations.

Government officials saw no conflict. Indeed, the superintendent's annual report of 1904 stated that "the new mining village of Bankhead, instead of being a detriment to the beauty of the Park will, on the contrary, add to its many and varied attractions." Though parks had grown larger, the concept that they should pay their way continued as a pillar of park philosophy. The concept of wilderness preservation was a distant notion.

This was most apparent in the attitudes concerning wildlife. The Victorian concept of nature as being either good or evil did not permit the

Storage dam at outlet of Lake Minnewanka, ca. 1912—15.

Coal mines at Bankhead, ca. 1912. Bankhead was once a thriving mining town of 900 people. Established in 1903, the mine employed 275 men below ground and 195 above. The town was owned and operated by the C.P.R. and was noted for the very best in service. Poor quality coal and competition from mines in Canmore, Drumheller, and Lethbridge forced the closure of the Bankhead mines in 1922. The town disappeared soon after.

preservation ethic to extend beyond certain species. A park directive clearly illustrates this fact: "The Superintendent will let nature alone as much as possible...at the same time, he will endeavor to exterminate all those animals which prey upon others." Today this is not regarded as an ecologically sound policy, but ecology was a term which did not become prevalent until the mid-twentieth century.

The conservation movement did have one very distinct benefit. Park boundaries were greatly increased—so much so that Canada became the first country in the world to set up a specific agency to control park lands, the Dominion Parks Branch. The choice of the first commissioner was fortuitous.

A NEW DIRECTION

J. B. HARKIN HAD very distinct notions about national parks. From the first he believed that these lands should be used primarily for recreation and education in a wilderness setting, and that resource industries had no place in parks. Recognizing that established patterns of use did not change overnight, Harkin embarked upon a major public relations campaign to convince politicians and the public that a new direction was in order. His efforts were greatly aided by a new invention—the automobile.

The great hegemony of the railway had been broken. No longer were the western parks accessible only by means of rail, nor was the clientele limited to those of greater financial means. Parks were opening up to the entire population—and with greater industrialization in the cities, the natural beauty and relaxation of the wilderness was becoming more and more attractive.

Public attitudes began to change. As resource industries were gradually phased out, there was a much greater emphasis upon recreational facilities, such as golf courses, tennis courts, dance halls, formal gardens, swimming pools, ski facilities, and manicured beaches. Townsites were opened up and leases were issued to build homes and summer cottages.

The results of Harkin's work were ultimately enshrined in The National Parks Act of 1930:
> "The parks are hereby dedicated to the people of Canada for their benefit, enjoyment, and education...and such parks shall be made use of so as to leave them unimpaired for the enjoyment of future generations."

As part of this major realignment in philosophy, Rocky Mountains Park became Banff National Park.

The National Parks Act was an important step. Its policy stressed that resource exploitation was not to be permitted within National Parks. For the first time in history, the protection of lands for future generations was stressed as strongly as the benefit to the present generation.

The trend towards preservation as the underlying ethic of National Parks continues. Today we recognize that there are some 48 natural regions in

Banff Avenue, 1926.

Canada, and it is the goal of the Parks Branch to protect representative samples of each.

The development of a national parks philosophy has been a long and fascinating journey. Today Banff represents all phases of this evolution. The townsite, the swimming facilities, the ski hills, the golf course, the ruins of the Bankhead Coal Mines, and the hydroelectric developments at Lake Minnewanka all represent various stages in the evolution of the park concept.

Most important of all, Banff represents the preservation of one of the most dramatic landscapes in Canada and the world—the Rocky Mountains of the Canadian Cordillera.

This legacy must be treated with respect and infinite care...a wilderness heritage to pass on to future generations.

Raspberry Bay,
Lake Minnewanka,
ca. late 1800s.

No scene better symbolizes the mountain legacy protected by national parks than Lake Louise. The small cabin to the right in the above photo was the original Lake Louise Hotel.

Containing only two bedrooms, a kitchen, and a sitting room, the chalet was a far cry from the opulent chateau which replaced the small wood building.

THE MOUNTAIN LEGACY

THE ROCKY MOUNTAINS afford some of the most spectacular scenery to be found anywhere in the world. Within the 6,670 square kilometres of Banff's boundaries can be found two of the cordillera's mountain zones: the Front Ranges and the Main Ranges. Each zone has its own distinctive appearance and characteristics.

For over a billion years, sediments accumulated, layer upon layer, in a deep ocean basin. Scientists theorize that about 200 million years ago, as the volume of sediments increased, the earth began a process of major readjustment. The massive plates which comprise the surface of the earth began to change their direction of movement. The plate

containing North America, which had previously been moving east, reversed its direction and ploughed back into the sedimentary basin. So intense was the compression that blocks of sediments 12,000 to 15,000 metres thick were lifted, folded, faulted, and transported up to 200 kilometres from the original point of deposition in a process that moved from west to east.

The deepest and oldest part of the ocean depression—the first to be uplifted—became the Main Ranges. Because of thick deposits of sand and gravel, the sediments were only gently warped into large-scale upfolds and downfolds. Thus, the strata retain a generally horizontal position, giving the Main Ranges their "layer cake" appearance.

The shallower, newer part of the ocean basin did not have the deposits of sand and gravel and reacted quite differently to the stress of mountain building. These limestones and shales were severely disrupted. In some areas the rock layers were actually folded back on themselves. In other areas, the sheets of stone were lifted and pushed upon one another piggy-back style, like shingles on a roof. Thus, much of the Front Ranges are characterized by steep faces and sloping backs.

The process of mountain building was slow, with each pulse of movement limited to only a few centimetres per year. As each massive slice of sediments was forced upward, it was immediately challenged by the erosive power of water. The top layers of sediments were stripped away, exposing more ancient pages of earth's history. Since the Main Ranges were the first of Banff's mountains to be born, the erosive effect of water acted upon the rock mass for a longer period of time. These mountains thus reveal the oldest sections of Banff's story.

Rivers and streams born in the Main Ranges gradually dissected the rock sheets into the primitive precursors of today's mountains. One particular stream played an extraordinary role in the history of this country. That river was the early Bow River.

Virtually all other rivers in the area became trapped between the stone wedges. But the Bow River had sufficient strength to cut into the sheets of stone at the same pace the Front Ranges were rising. As a result the Bow River became one of the few passages into the mountains from the plains. It was this valley which was ultimately selected by the Canadian Pacific Railway in its bid to bind the nation of Canada from sea to sea. And it was the financial requirements of the railway and the discovery of a few rather insignificant looking springs which led to the creation of a new concept—national parks.

The rugged beauty of these mountains is a relatively recent experiment in terms of geological history. When water acts as the major erosive force, mountains tend to be more rounded. Rivers are abundant, lakes are not. Several million years ago, however, temperatures grew cold enough to permit the establishment of vast icefields along the continental divide. From these accumulation points, rivers of ice flowed into the valley corridors, the most important of which were the valleys of the Athabasca, North Saskatchewan, and the Bow systems.

The effect was dramatic. Water-carved, V-shaped valleys were widened and steepened into broad U-shapes. Valley walls were at times undermined with resultant rock slides. The freeze-thaw of the colder temperatures caused blocks of stone to be broken from the mountain front, thereby establishing the rough angular forms familiar today. Where ice was deepest and most active, massive basins were hewn from the bedrock cresting the spectacular valley lakes. On a smaller scale, ice which formed in depressions on mountainsides above the flow of the valley glaciers carved tiny alpine bowls called cirques. Several of these cirque glaciers would often chew at the same summit, resulting in turretlike, or pyramidal, mountain peaks.

(Facing page) Glaciers once covered the Canadian Cordillera, leaving only a few isolated peaks towering above a sea of ice. Today, glaciers remain in isolated pockets, the most notable being the Columbia Icefield.

LIFE IN BANFF

THE MOMENTS, THOUGH often fleeting, sparkle as vivid memories: the early morning mist rising from the still lake waters, the plunge of the osprey, the heart-stopping crash of wapiti through the forest, the delicate fragrance of an alpine meadow.

As with any nature experience, a true appreciation of the mountains cannot be rushed. You need patience and a willingness to relax your pace.

The diversity of the valley bottom allows the visitor the easiest opportunity to adjust to the slower pace. At elevations below 1,370 metres the environment is much drier. Only slight changes in soil drainage, sunshine, or wind are required to dramatically alter the ecological community. Abrupt shifts from dense stands of spruce and subalpine fir to pockets of grassland or open savannah forests of Douglas-fir are not uncommon. This mosaic of environments supports a wealth of quite different plants and animals in a very small area. As a result, one need not travel far or have undue patience to sight many of the residents of the valley.

The grasslands of the dry, south-facing slopes are characteristic of the valley bottom where larger animals, such as wapiti, sheep, and deer gather. These pockets of grassland are critical to their survival during the harsh winter season. Only here on these windswept slopes are snows sufficiently shallow to permit easy access to food supplies.

Somewhat less obvious are the smaller residents of the valley bottom. Colonies of Columbia ground squirrels which reside in the more open areas remain constantly on guard for coyotes and hawks, their chief enemies. Virtually all grassland residents have the dusty brown colour of their environment to avoid detection. In contrast, the saucy black and white magpie seems a little too obvious. However, there is a logic to this "clown's" appearance. The stark black and white coloration makes it virtually invisible in the light and shadow environment of the poplar forests where it often builds its nests.

Top to bottom: deer, Columbia ground squirrel, moose.

(Facing page) The valley floor is a rich mosaic of environments including deciduous forest, coniferous forest, grassland, and marshland.

19

Indian paintbrush.

Gray jay.

(Facing page) The subalpine is the largest ecological zone in the park, encompassing the extensive coniferous forests which cloak the mountain slopes. The subalpine is noted for a wide range of flowers, which creates spectacular natural gardens.

Greater patience is required in the subalpine. In the oldest spruce-fir forests the great interlocking branches steal most of the light from the forest floor. As a result, little ground vegetation is available for the larger animals, and only a few year-round residents call the mature forest their home. Skittish red squirrels, pine martens, and spruce grouse are seen rarely. Indeed, it is most often the alarm chatter of the squirrel which indicates its presence.

When fire has devastated a mature forest, however, a transitional lodgepole pine forest quickly takes its place. Living for only a few hundred years before the spruce and fir can reestablish itself, the lodgepole pine forest has a more open canopy which permits greater sunlight to reach the forest floor. The understory is much richer. In these transitional forests black bear, deer, sheep, and elk seek food and shelter during the summer months.

Two gray black birds break the rule concerning the need for stealth and patience. The gray jay and the Clark's nutcracker have a tendency to seek you out rather than vice versa. The unofficial name of the gray jay, "camp robber," indicates why these are often the most commonly sighted residents.

21

The alpine requires the most patience. In this cold, harsh environment all plant life must seek the safety of the ground to escape the drying winds and the cutting ice. In a treeless land, motion spells danger. As a result, most residents use camouflage and an ability to freeze at a moment's notice as their primary means of defence.

Rest quietly along an alpine trail and simply gaze over what at first appears to be an empty, barren, rocky meadow. Your patience will usually be rewarded. When the residents feel secure, motion resumes. What first appeared to be a pile of boulders suddenly becomes the focus of activity for the tiny pika, which gathers, cures, and stores cut vegetation as a form of hay, and the larger, lazier marmot, which relies on its fat deposits to support it through its winter hibernation. Even when moving, the master of camouflage, the ptarmigan, remains difficult to locate. Often you must rely on the soft

Mountain goat, hoary marmot, moss campion.

(Facing page) The alpine is the harshest of the mountain ecological zones, and most plants grow close to the ground to avoid the wind and cold.

clucking of the parent to locate this alpine grouse and its brood of fluffy chicks.

While the larger mammals such as the caribou, sheep, and wapiti are easily seen in the stark meadows, quiet and stealth remain important to prevent a hasty retreat by these animals into the next meadow.

If you see the master of the wilderness, however, leave immediately. The grizzly is both powerful and potentially dangerous when surprised.

THE SPRINGS

THOUGH SOMEWHAT insignificant to our eyes today, these springs were a "hot" property a hundred years ago. Hot mineral springs meant curative waters. Curative waters permitted the creation of resorts. Resorts spelled visitors and revenue for the Canadian Pacific Railway. And the survival of the railway meant the survival of a young country called Canada. In terms of this country's history these springs are not at all insignificant.

All the springs originate as surface waters which seep through fractures created during mountain building. The deeper the fissures, the warmer the waters become and the greater the capacity to dissolve a substantial quantity of minerals. When the waters reach an impermeable layer (estimated to be as deep as several thousand metres) they are forced to the surface through another series of channels. As the waters cool, the minerals are released and redeposited as the friable stone called tufa.

Each spring has its own characteristic flow volume, chemical composition, and temperature. It is common for the temperature to fluctuate throughout the year depending upon the volume of

The Cave and Basin swimming complex.

Although the Cave once had stalactites hanging from the ceiling and walls, early generations of souvenir hunters have gradually removed them, piece by piece.

water entering the system and the rate at which the water is recycled. On occasion the temperatures will drop significantly for a long period of time. When this occurs the rate of deposition of minerals is superseded by the gradual removal of the stone through erosion.

Such a cooling occurred in the Cave and Basin Springs. It was the gradual eating back of the minerals which resulted in the distinctive shapes of the basins which hold the mineral waters. Originally the only entrance into the Cave was through the small hole in the top of the dome. Early park visitors were forced to descend to the pool by means of ladders until the present passage was blasted into the Cave in 1887.

Two swimming and soaking complexes are located at the Upper Hot Springs and at the Cave and Basin Springs. The latter facility, originally constructed in 1914, has been completely refurbished and redeveloped as part of the 1985 Parks Canada centennial celebrations. As part of this redevelopment, a replica of the original bath house has been constructed near the Basin springs.

THE TOWNSITE AREA

THERE HAVE BEEN numerous towns within the borders of Banff National Park. Bankhead was a coal mining village; Siding 29 was a railway support town. There was the resort village of Minnewanka, and the mining community of Silver City—a town that for a few brief years rivalled early Calgary in terms of growth.

Only one community remains. Beginning as a support centre for the spas and springs, Banff townsite was designed to provide the best of services and facilities for its visitors. By 1900 Banff boasted eight luxury hotels, a myriad of coach roads leading to the surrounding natural features, dozens of shops, and excellent recreational facilities. For much of its early history, Banff was recognized primarily as a summer resort. By 1910, however, the C.P.R. and the government were advertising Banff as a winter playground. As demand increased, the town improved its older facilities as exemplified by the construction of the Cave and Basin buildings and the expansion of the Banff Springs Hotel.

There were no restrictions on who could live in Banff, and as a result there was an explosion in the number of summer cottages. In 1933 the establishment of the Banff School of Fine Arts added a major cultural centre to this growing community.

The passage of the National Parks Act in 1930 demanded a limit to the growth of the town. As park philosophy changed, it became apparent that uncontrolled growth would compromise the preservation ethic of the Parks Act. Today Banff administrators must manage a tourist centre that

Upper terminal of the Gondolas at the summit of Sulphur Mountain.

attracts millions of people each year.

For a century Banff has sustained the tradition of offering opulence and luxury at the threshold of wilderness, and it continues to take great pride in presenting to the world an extraordinary array of natural wonders that ring the town like gems.

(Facing page) View of Banff townsite from Sulphur Mountain.

A small representative herd of bison remain in the Buffalo Paddock.

Hoodoos on Tunnel Mountain.

(Facing page) Banff Springs Hotel.

Mount Rundle seen from the air, and reflected in Vermilion Lake.

LAKE MINNEWANKA DRIVE

MINNEWANKA IS A Cree Indian name meaning "Lake of the Water Spirit." If such a spirit does exist this would be the appropriate location. Lake Minnewanka, at 19 kilometres in length, is the largest and deepest of Banff's glacial lakes. Nestled between the spectacular Palliser and Fairholme ranges, the lake offers a passage deep into the park's northern wilderness.

Beneath the icy waters of the lake rest the remains of the small resort village of Minnewanka that flourished around the turn of the century. It was abandoned when the decision was made in 1912 to dam the outflow of the lake to provide electricity for Banff. When more electricity was required after the demise of the coal mining community of Bankhead, a new powerhouse was constructed in 1924. Finally, in 1941, as part of the war effort, the dam was greatly expanded to provide even more electricity. As a result of these hydroelectric developments, the depth of the lake was increased some 23 metres.

Views of Lake Minnewanka.

BANKHEAD

Rocky Mountain bighorn sheep.

THE RUINS OF THE mining community of Bankhead are a reminder of the development philosophy of early park management. Originally established to provide a local source of coal from Cascade Mountain for the railway, the town grew rapidly after the opening of the mine in 1903.

Bankhead was the pride of the government and the C.P.R. Not only did the mines produce half a million tonnes of coal annually, and employ close to 500 men, the town itself had some of the most modern facilities available anywhere. There were two dairies, a butcher, baker, laundries, general stores, a church, school, and recreational facilities such as a skating rink and curling rink. Services included electricity, running water, and sewers.

Despite the high thermal quality, the coal was severely broken. The railway had to import pitch from Pennsylvania to compress the coal dust and fragments into briquettes. The high cost of production and a series of labour strikes spelled disaster for the town. On June 15, 1922, the mine was closed.

Silver City was a short-lived boom town dependent upon poor grade ores. Only a Parks Canada display now marks the site of the village.

(Facing page) Castle Mountain.

THE BOW VALLEY PARKWAY

TIRED OF THE FAST pace of the Trans-Canada Highway? The Bow Valley Parkway offers a relaxing alternative. The roadway has been completely redeveloped to provide numerous picnic sites, viewpoints, and interpretive displays for visitors wishing a leisurely passage between Banff and Lake Louise.

One of the more intriguing sites along the Parkway is located soon after you begin the journey from Banff. As the name implies there is indeed a "hole in the wall" of Mt. Cory. It is believed that this is part of an old underground cave system that has been exposed by glacial action.

This channel is representative of a number of cave systems which have been carved from the limestones of the Rocky Mountains. Percolating water, following cracks and fissures in the stone, joined with carbon dioxide to create a weak acid. This acid is the primary force behind the intricate networking of channels that honeycombs many of these mountains.

Perhaps the most distinctive of all the mountains between Banff and Lake Louise is Castle Mountain, located near Johnston Canyon.

According to native legend, this spectacular 2,862 metre mountain is the home of the chinook—the warm wind which sweeps out of the mountains and onto the plains in late winter. Chinooks are created from air masses which first rise rapidly over the mountains and lose most of their moisture. Then, as the air rapidly descends, it is warmed. The only obstruction in this valley, Castle Mountain forces valley winds to ascend very abruptly. The air is cooled quickly with elevation and clouds stream from the summit. The result is that Castle Mountain appears to be creating the chinook directly at its peak.

By its appearance Castle Mountain is appropriately named. Scientifically it is classified as a *castleate* mountain. As the softer layers of stone erode, the harder, more resistant layers are undermined. Massive rockfalls result, ensuring the maintenance of these steep mountain fronts.

Once a small town rested in the shadow of this great mountain. In 1881 a Stoney Indian showed prospector J. J. Healy a piece of iron ore rich in silver and copper. The news spread rapidly, and as soon as the railway entered the region in 1883, over a thousand men swarmed to the site.

Log cabins, stores, brickyards, a lime kiln, and four mines immediately sprang to life. The quality of the ore was poor, however. No silver was ever found and the copper, lead, and zinc deposits were uneconomical.

By 1885 Silver City was nothing more than a memory.

JOHNSTON CANYON

LET YOUR IMAGINATION roam. Try to envision a picture of these mountains that is quite different from today's reality. Imagine a scene of rounded water-washed mountains deeply dissected by very steep valleys with precipitous walls. Mountains seem to be packed more closely together and the valleys are narrower. Torrential rivers and streams abound; lakes are rare.

What you have imagined is the landscape that existed for most of the life of the Rocky Mountains. Prior to the glacial age, water was the most important force of erosion. During the ice ages, when the ice sheets advanced, then retreated, several times, valleys were widened and the mountains were made more rugged and angular.

The deep canyon walls, the churning cauldrons of water, and the mists of Johnston Canyon represent the resurgent power of water since the retreat of the glaciers approximately 10,000 years ago. Following weaknesses in the stone, Johnston Creek has cut rapidly into these limestone sediments. The scene before you is a reminder of what was once the greatest sculpting tool in these mountains—water.

Parks Canada has constructed a unique trail at Johnston Canyon. Pathways are bolted directly above the creek, offering a rare opportunity to intimately experience the explosive power of water. These pathways also allow you to search for a strange little resident of the mountain streams—a small, plump, gray bird with a penchant for bobbing up and down. The water ouzel, or dipper, as it is more commonly known, builds its nest of mosses directly on the canyon wall. So thoroughly adapted to these streams is the dipper that it uses its wings to swim underwater, as well as to fly.

Johnston Canyon is an excellent example of the erosive power of water. Initiated only 10,000 years ago, after the retreat of the glaciers from this valley, Johnston Creek has managed to chip, scour, dissolve, and abrade the bedrock to create this impressive chasm.

LAKE LOUISE

DURING THE EVENING hours of August 23, 1882, distant rumblings echoed through the valleys around a survey camp. Tom Wilson, a packer for the C.P.R., questioned the Stoney Indian guides and was told that the thunder quite regularly arose from the "Lake of Little Fishes." Curiosity compelled Wilson to explore the source of the noise. He was ill prepared for the scene which awaited him.

It was, as he stated later, the most beautiful vision he had encountered throughout his many mountain journeys. Eleven mountains cradled the peaceful calm of an emerald green jewel. Reflected in the icy waters of the lake were the sources of the lake's thunder—the vast glaciers which clung to the steep slopes of towering Mt. Victoria and Mt. Lefroy. Collapsing blocks of ice from these glaciers reverberated throughout the valley.

Wilson immediately reported his discovery to the C.P.R. Although a railway station called Laggan was built 6.5 kilometres distant in 1883, it was not until 1890 that the first modest wooden hotel facility was constructed at the lake. It had but two bedrooms, a kitchen, and a large sitting room. Fire destroyed the building two years later. Rebuilt in 1893 the structure was expanded in 1900 and again in 1913. Once again disaster struck. Fire claimed the Chalet in 1924. The following year the Chateau of today was built.

Lake Louise was well known for its opportunities for climbing, hiking, canoeing, and horseback riding. Whereas Banff was known for opulence and elegance, Lake Louise seemed to provide a touch more freedom and exuberance for its guests. For example, the C.P.R., somewhat exasperated with a few of its patrons, finally had to install revolving doors to stop riders on horseback from entering the lobby.

It is highly recommended that visitors take the 6.5 kilometre Plain-of-Six-Glaciers Trail to gain a spectacular view of the Victoria glacier. It was this glacier which left the large wall of broken rock rubble that dams the lake. If you wish to obtain a more overall picture of the area, the Lake Louise gondolas, situated across the valley, will take you to the 2,043-metre summit of Mt. Whitehorn.

Though appearing deceptively small when viewed from the Chateau, Lake Louise is actually eight kilometres long and two and a half kilometres wide. This aerial view of the lake and Chateau Lake Louise shows clearly the impressive size of the glacial lake.

MORAINE LAKE—
VALLEY OF THE TEN PEAKS

Moraine Lake has many moods. It takes only minor changes in weather or sunlight to alter the colour of the lake and the atmosphere of the valley.

IF ANY SCENE CAN challenge the beauty of Lake Louise it is Moraine Lake in the Valley of the Ten Peaks. Fed by the Wenkchemna (an Indian word for ten) Glacier, Moraine Lake appears at first as simply a smaller version of Lake Louise.

In contrast to the tranquil serenity which pervades the scene at Lake Louise, however, the close proximity of the ten towering mountain sentinels adds a fierce ruggedness to the picture at Moraine Lake. The mountains seem less hospitable, and there is a sense of the awesome powers involved in the creation of this landscape.

These are the Main Ranges. The mountains of this zone are characterized by relatively flat-lying sediments, in contrast to the steeply inclined layers in the Front Ranges near Banff. The lower reddish brown base to these mountains is the compressed sand and gravel of an ancient range of mountains that once stood in northern Canada over a billion years ago. They were dismantled and redistributed in the ocean basin as the layers called *gog quartzites*.

Around 600 million years ago, calcium carbonate, produced by sea life, became the major form of sediment. Compressed into limestone these deposits constitute the grayish upper half of the Main Ranges.

Moraine Lake does differ from Lake Louise in one major way. Whereas Lake Louise is dammed by a glacial moraine, Moraine Lake is blocked by the remains of two major rockfalls from the 2,314-meter Tower of Babel.

THE ICEFIELD PARKWAY

FROM RIVER VALLEY to alpine summit, the Icefield Parkway offers views so spectacular and so commanding that this roadway has been classified as one of the most beautiful scenic routes in the world. Do not rush this trip. Take time for exploration. You will be rewarded for your efforts.

Throughout your journey you will be flanked by an unbroken but constantly changing chain of mountains. From Lake Louise you remain within the Main Ranges. As you enter the Parkway from the Trans-Canada Highway you pass the oldest stone known in this area—layers of compressed sands and gravels that were deposited over a billion years ago. The closer you get to the Columbia Icefield, the younger the rock becomes in terms of geological age. These are the limestones which were deposited during the age of massive coral reefs which thrived in shallow sea waters. As your journey continues to Jasper you drop once again through time.

As you progress along the Parkway, particularly in the vicinity of the Bow Summit, look to the strata, or rock layers, in the mountains on each side of the valley. Notice how the rock layers dip at an angle. In your mind's eye, trace the layers from one side of the valley to the other. This massive dome you have created provides a graphic illustration of an anticline and the broad-scale upfolding of rock strata which occurs during mountain building.

During the gentle "warping" of the rock, the top of the anticline was strained and cracked to a greater degree than the rock at the edges of the dome. It was along these lines of weakness that erosion was most effective, carving a valley from the broken crest of this extraordinary wedge of stone.

Vast rivers of ice once filled this valley. Their action and movement created the broad, gentle U-shape that is visible today. Glacial fields remain localized in the valleys to the south where colder, moister climatic conditions offer safe havens.

On occasion very localized climatic conditions permit smaller glaciers to survive far from the icefields. Such is the case with the spectacular

The Icefield Parkway, showing the mountain strata.

Crowfoot Glacier.

Crowfoot glacier. This is a cliff glacier. The bench of stone upon which the majority of the glacier rests is fairly resistant to erosion. The strata directly above it, however, is less resistant. The ice continues to scour and pluck at this weaker strata, thereby increasing the size of its own little haven on the precipitous cliffs.

Glaciers are very sensitive to minute changes in climate. When the Crowfoot glacier was first named it had three very distinct branches. Because of a slight change in climate in recent decades the lowest of the claws has disappeared. The other two

Tons of pulverized stone known as "glacial flour" are released into the lakes by the glacial meltwaters. This produces the spectacular colours of the lakes of the Parkway. The best-known example is Peyto Lake (below), named after the mountain guide Bill Peyto, who explored the region in 1894.

branches remain healthy.

Of all the remarkable sights along the Parkway, none is more breathtaking than the extraordinary iridescent colours of the glacial lakes. The solution to the mystery of what creates these magnificent shades of turquoise rests with the glaciers that supply the lake water. As glaciers move they grind bedrock into fine powder known as glacial flour. Carried by meltwater streams to the lakes, this material is so fine that much remains suspended in solution. It is the reaction of sunlight to the fine particles which creates the colours of the lakes.

One need only think of a rainbow to remember that sunlight is actually composed of a myriad of wavelengths that we see as colours. When sunlight enters water without any particles, the red, orange, and yellow wavelengths are rapidly absorbed by the

surface waters. Greens are absorbed at a little more depth, leaving only blue to be reflected back to our eyes.

In glacial lakes something a little different occurs. The reds, oranges, and yellows are again quickly absorbed at the surface. The glacial flour in turn rapidly absorbs the blue wavelengths. As a result, only the green remains as the primary colour that is sent back to us.

Where streams flow into the lake the amount of sediment is so great and so close to the surface that occasionally the surface water does not even absorb the yellow wavelength. As a result, yellow green splashes of colour often play across these turquoise pools.

Waterfowl Lake.

(Below) Lake Louise.

COLUMBIA ICEFIELD

IT IS THE CROWNING glory of the Parkway:
a 385-square kilometre cap of glacial ice nestled in
some of the highest mountains of the Rockies. The
high elevation keeps temperatures sufficiently cold
and captures enough moisture to sustain the
Columbia Icefield and its tributary glaciers.

The largest icefield in the Rockies is also the
birthplace of three of Canada's major river systems.
The Athabasca River joins the Mackenzie to flow to
the Arctic Ocean; the Saskatchewan River flows
across the plains to Lake Winnipeg and then to
Hudson's Bay; and the Columbia River flows
through British Columbia and the United States to
the Pacific Ocean.

The most accessible of the glaciers is the
Athabasca. Snowmobile tours allow visitors access to
this 7-kilometre-long, 305-metre-thick river of ice.

Athabasca Glacier.

Unless accompanied by trained personnel, you should not approach a glacier. The ice moves constantly and poses many dangers, including crevasses up to 60 metres deep, drainage tunnels, called millwells, which lead from the surface of the glacier deep into its interior, and ice caves and ice blocks which can collapse without warning.

Technically, the Athabasca glacier is in Jasper National Park. To see Banff's most famous representative you must hike the trail called Parker's Ridge. The switchbacks lead past old fossilized coral reefs and exquisite alpine gardens. Once at the summit you are treated to an aerial view of the 11-kilometre-long Saskatchewan glacier. Parker's Ridge is also one of the few locations close to a resident population of mountain goat.

Copyright ©1986 by Whitecap Books Ltd.

Canadian Cataloguing in Publication Data

Bondar, Barry
  Banff chronicles

  ISBN 0-920620-94-9
  1. Banff Region (Alta.) - History. 2.
Banff Region (Alta.) - Description and
travel - Guide-books. 3. Banff Region
(Alta.) - Description and travel - Views.
I. Title.
FC3695.B5B65 1986 917.123'3 C86-091229-9
F1079.B5B65 1986

Typeset by The Typeworks, Vancouver, B.C.

Printed by D.W. Friesen & Sons, Altona, Manitoba, Canada

Published by Whitecap Books, 1086 W. 3rd Street, North
Vancouver, B.C.

Photo Credits

Front cover: John Burridge, Photo/Graphics
Back cover: Glenbow Museum, NA-2755-6
pp. 2—14: Glenbow Museum
    p.2: NA-637-6; p.3: NA-1097-4; p.4: NA-531-2; p.5:
    bottom: NA-2126-19, top: NA-4465-43; p.6: NA-
    2977-37; p.7: NA-529-23; p.8: NA-345-2; p.9: top:
    NA-3551-73, bottom: NA-237-38; p.10: NA-3544-22;
    p.11: NA-612-1; p.12/13: NA-554-2; p.13: NA-2977-
    14; p.14 top: NA-2977-17, bottom: NA-2977-27.

pp.15: Barry Bondar; p.17: Bob Herger, Photo/Graphics; p.18:
Travel Alberta; p.19 top and bottom: Terry Willis; p.19 middle:
Derek and Jane Abson, Photo/Graphics; p.20: Bob Herger,
Photo/Graphics; p.21 top right and bottom: Roger Laurilla,
Photo/Graphics; p.21 top left: Gunter Marx, Photo/Graphics; p.22
left: Roger Laurilla, Photo/Graphics; p.22 bottom: Derek and Jane
Abson, Photo/Graphics; p.22 top right: Barry Bondar; p.23: Fred
Chapman, Photo/Graphics; p.24/25: Roger Laurilla,
Photo/Graphics; p.26: Gunter Marx, Photo/Graphics; p.27,28 top:
Travel Alberta; p.28 bottom left: Roger Laurilla, Photo/Graphics,
bottom right: John Burridge, Photo/Graphics; pp.29,30 bottom:
Derek and Jane Abson, Photo/Graphics; p.30 top: John Burridge,
Photo/Graphics; p.31, John Burridge, Photo/Graphics; p.32 top:
Barry Bondar; p.32 bottom: Gunter Marx, Photo/Graphics; p.33 top:
Terry Willis, Photo/Graphics; p.33 bottom: John Burridge,
Photo/Graphics; p.34: Glenbow Museum, NA-160-1; p.35: Gunter
Marx, Photo/Graphics; pp.36,37: Travel Alberta; p.38: Bob Herger,
Photo/Graphics; p.39: Michael Burch; p.40: Bob Herger,
Photo/Graphics; p.41: John Burridge, Photo/Graphics; p. 42:
Gunter Marx, Photo/Graphics; p.43: Travel Alberta; p.44: Gunter
Marx, Photo/Graphics; p.45 top: Bob Herger, Photo/Graphics; p.45
bottom: Jurgen Vogt, Photo/Graphics; p.46 top: Roger Laurilla,
Photo/Graphics; p.46 bottom, p.47 top: Barry Bondar; p.47 bottom:
Travel Alberta; p.48 Barry Bondar.